# Little Big Giant

### Stories of Wisdom and Inspiration

# Introduction

As the sun set over the vast empire of Alexander the Great, the young conqueror stood atop a hill, surveying the land he had fought so hard to claim. With his piercing blue eyes and unruly blonde hair, he exuded a sense of power and determination that was unmatched by any other ruler of his time. But as he gazed out at the sprawling cities and villages below, a sudden realization struck him - his thirst for conquest was insatiable, and he would stop at nothing to achieve his ultimate goal: world domination. Little did he know, this obsession would ultimately lead to his downfall, and cement his legacy as one of the most legendary and controversial figures in history.

# Table of Contents

# Chapter 1

*Childhood and Early Life: The Prince of Macedonia*

Alexander was born in 356 BC in the kingdom of Macedonia, located in the northern part of ancient Greece. His father, King Philip II, was a strong and powerful ruler who had big plans for his kingdom. Alexander's mother, Queen Olympias, was also a powerful figure who came from a long line of royal ancestors.

From a young age, Alexander showed great intelligence and curiosity. He was always asking questions and seeking knowledge, much to the delight of his tutors. He was also physically strong and had a natural talent for riding horses and using weapons.

As the son of a king, Alexander had access to the best education. He was taught by the famous philosopher Aristotle, who taught him about literature, philosophy, and politics. Alexander was a quick learner and absorbed everything like a sponge.

But despite his privileged upbringing, Alexander faced many challenges in his childhood. His father was often away on military campaigns, leaving Alexander and his mother to manage the kingdom. This taught Alexander the importance of leadership and responsibility from a young age.

One of the most significant events in Alexander's childhood was when he tamed a wild horse named Bucephalus. The horse had been deemed untamable by many, but

Alexander saw potential in him. He approached the horse calmly and managed to ride him, much to the amazement of everyone watching. This showed Alexander's determination and courage, traits that would serve him well in the future.

**Key Takeaway:** Alexander's childhood was filled with learning, responsibility, and challenges. It taught him valuable lessons about leadership, determination, and courage, which would shape him into the great leader he would become.

# Chapter 2

*The Rise to Power: Alexander's First*

*Battles*

Alexander was only 20 years old when he became the king of Macedonia. He was young, but he was determined to prove himself as a great leader. He had been trained in battle and strategy by his father, King Philip II, and he was ready to put his skills to the test.

Alexander's first battle was against the Thracian tribe, who had rebelled against Macedonia. With a small army, Alexander led his men into battle. He was fearless and brave, leading the charge himself. The Thracians were caught off guard by the young king's ferocity and were quickly defeated.

This victory gave Alexander and his army a boost of confidence. They were ready for their next challenge - the city of Thebes. Thebes was a powerful city-state and had a large army. But Alexander was determined to conquer it and show the world that he was a force to be reckoned with.

The battle of Thebes was fierce and lasted for months. But Alexander's army was well-trained and disciplined, and they were able to defeat the Thebans. Alexander showed mercy to the city, sparing the lives of its citizens. This act of kindness earned him the respect of the Greek city-states.

With Thebes under his control, Alexander set his sights on Persia. The Persian Empire was the largest and most powerful in the world at that time. Alexander's father had been planning to invade Persia, but he died before he could do so. Alexander saw it as his duty to fulfill his father's dream.

The Persian army was much larger than Alexander's, but he was not afraid. He had studied their tactics and knew their weaknesses. In the battle of Granicus, Alexander led his army to victory, defeating the Persians and gaining control of their territory.

Alexander's next target was the city of Tyre. Tyre was an island city, surrounded by water and protected by high walls. Many thought it was impossible to conquer, but Alexander was determined. He built a causeway to connect the island to the mainland and launched a surprise attack. The city fell after a seven-month siege, and Alexander became known as the conqueror of Tyre.

**Key Takeaway:** Even though Alexander was young, he was a skilled leader and strategist. He was fearless and determined, and he never gave up even when faced with seemingly impossible challenges. This shows that with hard work and determination, anything is possible.

# Chapter 3

*Conquering the Persian Empire: The Battle*

*of Issus*

As Alexander and his army marched further into the heart of the Persian Empire, they faced their biggest challenge yet - the mighty Persian army led by King Darius III. The two forces met at the Battle of Issus, a fierce clash that would determine the fate of the entire empire.

Alexander's army was outnumbered by the Persians, but they were determined to prove their strength and determination. The young king, only 25 years old, rode on his powerful horse Bucephalus, leading his troops into battle. He wore a shining suit of armor and carried a long spear, ready to face any enemy that came his way.

The Persians, on the other hand, were known for their skilled cavalry and fierce warriors. They were confident in their ability to defeat the Greeks and maintain their hold on the empire. But Alexander was not one to back down from a challenge.

As the two armies clashed, the sound of swords clashing and shields colliding echoed through the battlefield. Alexander's troops fought with all their might, using their superior tactics and discipline to hold their ground against the Persians. But the Persians were not easily defeated, and the battle raged on for hours.

In the midst of the chaos, Alexander spotted King Darius riding towards him, determined to take down the young king himself. Without hesitation, Alexander charged towards him, his spear aimed straight at the enemy king. The two engaged in a fierce duel, with Alexander's skill and agility proving to be a match for Darius' strength and experience.

As the battle raged on, Alexander's army slowly gained the upper hand. The Persians were no match for the Greeks' superior weaponry and tactics. In a final push, Alexander and his troops charged towards the Persian army, causing them to retreat in fear.

The Battle of Issus was a decisive victory for Alexander and his army. The Persians were no longer a threat, and the young king had proven his strength and leadership to his men. He showed great bravery and determination in the face of a formidable enemy, solidifying his place as one of the greatest military leaders in history.

**Key Takeaway:** Even when faced with overwhelming odds, determination and courage can lead to victory. Alexander's unwavering determination and bravery in the face of a powerful enemy is a lesson for all of us to never give up, no matter how difficult the challenge may seem.

# Chapter 4

## The Legendary Siege of Tyre

As Alexander the Great's army marched on, they encountered a mighty city known as Tyre. This city was like no other, for it was surrounded by the sea on all sides. The walls of Tyre were strong and tall, making it almost impenetrable. But Alexander was determined to conquer this city and add it to his growing empire.

The people of Tyre were not afraid of Alexander's army. They believed that their city was invincible and that no one could ever defeat them. But Alexander was not one to back down from a challenge. He knew that if he could conquer Tyre, it would show the world that he was truly a great leader.

Alexander's first attempt to conquer Tyre was through diplomacy. He sent messengers to the city, asking for their surrender. But the people of Tyre refused, mocking Alexander and his army. This only fueled Alexander's determination to conquer the city by force.

He ordered his army to build a causeway from the mainland to the island city of Tyre. This was no easy task, as the sea was deep and rough. But Alexander's army was skilled and determined. They worked day and night, using rocks and timber to build the causeway.

The people of Tyre were not idle during this time. They sent their ships to attack the causeway and set it on fire. But Alexander's army persevered, rebuilding the causeway each time it was destroyed. They even built towers on the causeway to protect themselves from the enemy ships.

Finally, after seven long months, the causeway was complete. Alexander's army marched across it and attacked the city of Tyre. The people of Tyre fought fiercely, but they were no match for Alexander's army. They were defeated and the city was conquered.

The fall of Tyre was a great victory for Alexander. It showed the world that he was a fearless and determined leader. But more importantly, it taught him the importance of perseverance and never giving up, even in the face of seemingly impossible challenges.

**Key Takeaway:** The siege of Tyre taught Alexander the Great the value of perseverance and determination. It also showed the world that even the mightiest cities can be conquered with hard work and determination.

# Chapter 5

*From Egypt to India: Alexander's*

*Expansion*

After conquering Persia and Egypt, Alexander the Great set his sights on expanding his empire even further. He had a burning desire to conquer the world and his next target was India.

With his army of loyal soldiers, Alexander marched through the scorching deserts of Egypt, facing many challenges along the way. The heat was unbearable and water was scarce, but Alexander's determination never wavered. He pushed his men to their limits, leading them through the treacherous terrain.

As they approached the banks of the Nile River, they were met with a fierce resistance from the Egyptian army. But Alexander was a master strategist and he quickly devised a plan to defeat them. He used his cavalry to outflank the enemy and launched a surprise attack, catching the Egyptians off guard. The battle was fierce, but in the end, Alexander emerged victorious.

With Egypt now under his control, Alexander continued his journey towards India. As he crossed the Arabian Sea, he encountered a massive storm that threatened to sink his ships. But Alexander's bravery and quick thinking saved his fleet from disaster.

Finally, they reached the shores of India and were met with a formidable opponent - King Porus. He had a strong army and was determined to defend his land against the invading Greeks. But Alexander was not one to back down from a challenge. He led his troops into battle, fighting fiercely against the Indian army.

The battle was long and bloody, but in the end, Alexander emerged victorious once again. King Porus was captured and Alexander showed him mercy, allowing him to continue ruling his kingdom under his authority.

With India now under his control, Alexander's empire stretched from Greece to India, making him one of the greatest conquerors in history. He had achieved what no one else had ever done before - conquering the known world.

**Key Takeaway:** Alexander the Great's determination, bravery, and strategic thinking were the key factors in his successful conquest of Egypt and India. He showed that with hard work and perseverance, anything is possible.

# Chapter 6

*The Battle of Gaugamela: Defeating the*

*Persian King Darius III*

Alexander the Great was on a mission to conquer the world. With his army of fearless soldiers, he had already conquered many lands and defeated powerful kings. But his ultimate goal was to defeat the mighty Persian Empire and its king, Darius III.

The two armies met on the plains of Gaugamela, a vast open field with no natural barriers to protect either side.

Darius III had a massive army of over 100,000 soldiers, while Alexander's army consisted of only 47,000 soldiers. But Alexander was not afraid. He had a brilliant plan and was determined to defeat Darius III once and for all.

As the sun rose on the day of the battle, Alexander's army was ready for the fight. They were well-trained and disciplined, with Alexander leading them at the front. On the other hand, Darius III's army was unorganized and lacked leadership.

The battle began with Darius III's chariots charging towards Alexander's army. But Alexander had prepared for this. He had instructed his soldiers to create gaps in their formation, allowing the chariots to pass through harmlessly. As the chariots passed, Alexander's soldiers closed the gaps, trapping the chariots and rendering them useless.

Next, Darius III's cavalry charged towards Alexander's army. But Alexander had a surprise for them. He had hidden a group of soldiers behind his army, and as the cavalry charged, they attacked from behind, causing chaos and confusion among Darius III's troops.

Despite their initial attacks, Darius III's army was no match for Alexander's well-planned tactics. Alexander's soldiers were fierce and determined, fighting with all their might. They were led by a fearless leader who inspired them to never give up.

As the battle raged on, Darius III realized that he was losing. In a desperate attempt to turn the tide, he fled from the battlefield, leaving his army behind. This was a significant blow to his soldiers' morale, and they soon surrendered, marking the end of the Persian Empire.

Alexander had achieved his ultimate goal. He had defeated Darius III and conquered the mighty Persian Empire. He was now the ruler of the largest empire in the world.

**Key Takeaway:** The Battle of Gaugamela teaches us that with proper planning, determination, and leadership, even the most significant challenges can be overcome. It also shows us the importance of adaptability and using our resources wisely in times of war.

# Chapter 7

## The Death of Alexander's Close Friend,

## Hephaestion

Alexander the Great had conquered many lands and built a vast empire, but he always had one constant companion by his side - his close friend, Hephaestion. They had grown up together and shared many adventures, battles, and triumphs. They were like brothers, always looking out for each other.

But one day, tragedy struck. Hephaestion fell ill and despite all efforts to save him, he passed away. Alexander was devastated. He had lost not only a close friend, but also a trusted advisor and confidant.

As Alexander mourned the loss of his dear friend, he couldn't help but feel a sense of guilt. He had pushed Hephaestion to join him on a journey to the city of Babylon, despite his friend's warnings of the dangerous climate. Alexander was determined to conquer the city and prove his strength and power. But in the end, it was Hephaestion who paid the ultimate price.

Alexander couldn't bear the thought of continuing his journey without his loyal friend by his side. He ordered a grand funeral for Hephaestion, with all the honors and rituals befitting a king. He even had a city named after him - Hephaestia - to honor his memory.

But even in death, Hephaestion's presence remained with Alexander. He would often visit his friend's tomb and hold conversations with him, seeking his advice and guidance. It was as if Hephaestion's spirit was still by his side, watching over him and guiding him on his conquests.

The death of Hephaestion was a turning point for Alexander. It made him realize the true cost of his ambition and conquests. He began to question the purpose of his conquests and whether it was worth sacrificing the lives of his loved ones.

**Key Takeaway:** The death of Hephaestion teaches us the importance of friendship and the consequences of ambition. It reminds us to value the people in our lives and not let our ambitions blind us to their well-being.

# Chapter 8

*The Mutiny at the Hyphasis River and the*

*Return to Babylon*

After conquering much of the known world, Alexander the Great and his army arrived at the Hyphasis River, which marked the eastern boundary of their conquests. Alexander was determined to continue his campaign and conquer more lands, but his army was exhausted and many of his soldiers had been away from their homes for years. They longed to return to their families and the comforts of their own land.

As they camped near the river, Alexander gathered his soldiers and shared his plans to continue their conquests. But to his surprise, his army refused to go any further. They were tired and homesick, and they had already conquered more lands than anyone thought possible. They demanded to return home.

Alexander was disappointed and frustrated, but he knew he couldn't force his soldiers to continue. Reluctantly, he agreed to turn back and return to Babylon, the capital of his empire.

The journey back was long and difficult. The weather was harsh and supplies were scarce. But Alexander refused to give up. He led his army through treacherous terrains, crossing rivers and mountains, and fighting off enemies along the way.

Despite the challenges, Alexander and his army finally arrived in Babylon. The city welcomed them with open arms, celebrating their victorious return. But Alexander's heart was heavy. He had hoped to conquer more lands and build a greater empire, but his army's mutiny had put an end to his dreams.

But even in defeat, Alexander showed great leadership. He didn't blame his soldiers for their mutiny, but instead, he thanked them for their bravery and sacrifices. He also showed great respect for the lands and people he had conquered, allowing them to keep their own customs and traditions.

**Key Takeaway:** Sometimes, even the greatest leaders face setbacks and have to change their plans. But true leadership is not about always winning, but about how we handle defeat and show respect for others.

# Chapter 9

*The Mysterious Death of Alexander the*

*Great*

Alexander the Great, the fearless conqueror and one of the greatest leaders in history, met his untimely death at the young age of 32. His sudden death has puzzled historians and scholars for centuries, with many theories surrounding the cause of his demise. Some say it was due to illness, while others believe it was a result of assassination. Let's delve into the mysterious death of this legendary ruler.

After conquering most of the known world, Alexander the Great was on his way back to Babylon, the capital of his empire. He had just defeated the Persian King Darius III and was looking forward to a peaceful reign. However, his journey was cut short when he fell ill with a high fever. Despite the best efforts of his physicians, his condition continued to worsen.

As his health deteriorated, Alexander's closest companions and generals gathered around him, hoping for his recovery. But on June 10th, 323 BC, Alexander took his last breath, leaving behind a legacy that would be remembered for centuries to come.

The cause of Alexander's death has been a subject of debate for many years. Some believe he died of malaria, a common illness in those times. Others speculate that he was poisoned by his enemies, as he had made many powerful enemies during his conquests. Some even say that he died due to heavy drinking, as he was known to indulge in alcohol.

One of the most popular theories surrounding Alexander's death is that he was a victim of typhoid fever. This theory is supported by the fact that many of his soldiers also fell ill with the same symptoms as him. However, there is no concrete evidence to prove this theory.

Another theory suggests that Alexander died due to a combination of factors, including alcohol, malaria, and a possible genetic disorder. It is believed that his father, King Philip II of Macedon, also died at a young age due to a similar illness.

Despite the numerous theories, the true cause of Alexander's death remains a mystery. His body was embalmed and placed in a golden coffin, but it was later stolen by Ptolemy I, one of his generals. The whereabouts of his body are still unknown.

**Key Takeaway:** The death of Alexander the Great is shrouded in mystery, with many theories surrounding the cause. It is a reminder that even the greatest leaders

are mortal and can be taken away from us
at any moment.

# Chapter 10

*Legacy and Impact: Alexander's Influence*

*on the World*

Alexander the Great was a remarkable leader and conqueror, but his legacy extends far beyond his military conquests. His influence on the world can still be seen and felt today, thousands of years after his death.

One of the most significant impacts of Alexander's conquests was the spread of

Greek culture and ideas throughout the known world. As he conquered different regions, he brought with him Greek language, art, and philosophy. This resulted in a blending of cultures and the birth of Hellenistic civilization, which would have a lasting impact on the world.

Alexander also left behind a legacy of great cities, many of which still exist today. He founded over 70 cities, including Alexandria in Egypt, which became a center of learning and trade. These cities served as hubs for cultural exchange and trade, further spreading Greek influence.

But perhaps Alexander's greatest impact was on the concept of leadership and empire building. He showed that a leader could unite diverse peoples and cultures under one rule, and his methods of organization and administration were studied and emulated by future leaders. He also introduced the concept of a "universal ruler," someone who could conquer and rule over the entire known world.

Another lasting legacy of Alexander is the spread of Christianity. As his empire expanded, so did the spread of Christianity, which would become the dominant religion in many of the regions he conquered. This had a profound impact on the world, shaping politics, culture, and society for centuries to come.

Alexander's influence on the world also extended to literature and art. His story and conquests inspired countless works of literature, including the famous epic poem, The Iliad. His image was also depicted in art, with many statues and paintings of him still existing today.

**Key Takeaway:** Alexander's legacy and impact on the world is undeniable. He spread Greek culture and ideas, founded great cities, and influenced the concept of leadership and empire building. His conquests also had a lasting impact on the spread of Christianity and inspired countless works of literature and art. His story continues to captivate and inspire people of all ages, making him one of the most influential figures in history.

# Dear Reader,

Thank you for choosing "Little Big Giant - Stories of Wisdom and Inspiration"! We hope this book has inspired and motivated you on your own journey to success.

If you enjoyed reading this book and believe in the power of its message, we kindly ask for your support. Please consider leaving a positive review on the platform where you purchased the book. Your review will help spread the message to more young readers, empowering them to dream big and achieve greatness. We acknowledge that mistakes can happen, and we appreciate your forgiveness.

Remember, the overall message of this book is the key. Thank you for being a part of our mission to inspire and uplift young minds.

Made in United States
Orlando, FL
15 December 2024

55823406R00049